I0470580

Easy Internet Entrepreneurialism

Steps To Creating Money Online

Todd Reinker

Table Of Contents

Introduction..4

Beyond Ordinary ...Accessing The 'Extra' ordinary When Devising A Website..9

One Example Of A Vision Statement....................................11

One Example Of A Mission Statement 14

Put That Train Into Motion..16

What Part Are You Playing? 21

Bridging The Gap Between What You Love And Making Others Love It Too...25

Focus: What Is Your Unique Blueprint? 32

Crucial Components For A Successful Business Plan 33

Capturing A Customer Following That Will Come Aboard Forever...39

Establishing Leaders 44

Company Goals: Setting And Fulfilling 48

Introduction

What Does Success Look Like For You?

Regardless of whether you are new to entrepreneurial adventures or you are a seasoned business professional with many years under your belt; you probably have your own definition of what success really looks like. Perhaps this image is ingrained deep within your quiet moments only to surface when you allow yourself to daydream. The bottom line is that it *is* still there and it *is* very crucial.

If you have no idea what success looks like, how can you possibly ever reach it? How can you create plans for it? How will you ever know if you are actually making advancments or simply getting by?

How Will You Know If You Have Reached Success?

This is something that you need to exercise with caution. Many people in this world simply define success as, "I am making two million dollars a year" and then leave it at that. Monetary goals are important, but they should only be a part of your plan of success. For some people, this is not even a part of their plan at all.

Picture your life as a successful person. What does it look like? Are you just sitting quietly in your beautiful home, or are you traveling all over the world?

Do you live in the busy city, or in a cabin tucked away in the mountains?

Are you working the usual 40 hours each week, or are you working a mere four hours each week?

What is it that you are doing? Are you planning things? Are you writing? Are you holding workshops? Are you talking to others on the phone? Are you creating something? How are you spending your time at work? Furthermore, how are you spending your free time?

Let us just assume that you are jotting down all of the things that you see when you visualize being successful. Now, what are your monetary goals? It is important to remember that while monetary goals are important, they are not the only definition of success. Every person has their own unique definition of success. Do not let your parents or society define it for you.

Building A Life That You Desire

Thanks to the internet, it is now possible for you to take your knowledge, passions and skills and share them with the world. If used properly, you can build the life that you deserve. This includes:

- Networking with others who are like minded
- Helping those in need
- Creating your own personal wealth
- Forging partnerships with others who have the same goals
- Enjoying life
- Learning new things from other people
- Sharing valuable skills and knowledge with those who need them
- Spending time doing the things with which you have passion

5

- And so much more

Using the internet you can create a business that is supportive of your goals, regardless of what your goals look like. There are many people that love their day jobs. They enjoy the people they work with and all of the benefits that come along with working a 9-5 job. An internet business will allow you to create the life that you truly desire by giving you the supplemental income that you need to take vacations, retire early, travel the world, or simply afford the little luxuries in life.

On the other hand, other people choose to make their internet business their full job. Their business becomes their primary source of income and allows them to afford to have the life that they deserve.

Of course, the question remains, How do you go from starting up an internet business to creating the life that you want? How do you actually achieve what you define as success?

Blueprint For Success

This is exactly what this book is designed to help you accomplish. The goal is to help you create your own blueprint for success. The term "blueprint" was chosen simply because every person has their own unique idea of what success is and their own methods for attaining it. If you are striving to have that four hour work week, your blueprint is going to look much different than someone who is striving for a 40 hour work week. Neither of these paths is wrong. Whether or not it is the right path for you will be dependent upon what your definition of success is, what you want in your life and what your vision is.

The biggest obstacle you will face is developing a plan that will help you reach that goal. The good news is that the process is not completely abstract. There are a number of steps that you can start taking today to reach the success you desire. As discussed earlier, the very first step you need to take is defining what success means to you. If you have not yet written down your own definition of success, then take a few minutes to sit down and write it now. Writing down your goals and aspirations is very helpful as it helps to keep you on the right track. It is so easy to get lost in the day to day world when trying to build a business. If you have your definition of success written down in front of you, it can help keep you focused and consider the bigger picture when making decisions.

Get to it! Take this moment to grab a piece of paper to write down your vision of success. If writing is not your strong suit and you would rather have a verbal record of your definition, you can grab a tape recorder and describe your personal vision of success. Describe what you are envisioning aloud. You can always refer to this recording later on, or have someone transcribe it for you.

Getting The Most Out Of This Book

It is advised that you only take on one chapter each day. This means that it should only take you a little over a week to complete your reading. If you would like, you can choose to go slower as well.

Each chapter will offer answers to some important questions and also provide you with some steps that you can start taking right away.

Please remember that this book is not a magical book that can provide you with all of the answers to your business questions. This book is simply designed to be a guide to help you create your own success.

It is best to avoid answering these questions in haste as they can really set you off course. You need to make sure that you think each question through and find an answer the fits your own definition of success and vision for success. This book is intended to provide you with a structure that can help you create a tremendous amount of wealth, but you must be willing to do the work. The book is merely the guide to help you find your way there. Remember:

- Read through each chapter thoroughly.
- Take your time so that you can digest the information, answer questions and brainstorm.
- Develop your own system that allows you to document all of your answers and your plans.
- Follow through with your plan and make an effort to keep documenting your progress.
- Start taking action and turning your vision into a reality using your plan as a guide.

Beyond Ordinary ...Accessing The 'Extra' ordinary When Devising A Website

With technology being so easily accessible today, just about everyone has a website of their own. The fitness guru that lives down the street may have his own blog where he shares his secret exercises and tips on how to create a fabulous workout program. A computer website developer may have his or her own site where they sell a how-to report. Just about everyone is in this business.

This is not that big of a deal. After all, they are not your competition.

They are simply owners of websites that felt that want to take part in the amazing medium that we call the internet. This is a medium that has substantially transformed the way we communicate and also the way that we do business.

A person who owns a website is simply someone who has decided that they want to make a mark in the world. They may have the aspiration to generate wealth online, but lack the resources and the tools to make this happen or the owner of the website may also be completely satisfied with the state of their website as is.

An entrepreneur and business owner, much like you, will have to go into this with a different perspective, set of goals and motivation. In this case, the goal is to create an entity that will be able to provide the type of lifestyle that you desire. To put it simply, what you want to do is create a business.

The owner of a website will take on many roles. They will serve as the CEO, the technical advisor, the supervisor and the writer. It will be their job to take on all of these tasks if and when they have time. On the other hand, this may really be more of a hobby for them.

Entrepreneur the Visionary

It may be true that you will take on many of these roles when your business is just getting started. The major difference is that you are working towards creating a business that suits your vision. You are creating plans that take advantage of your strengths. This means that you are also taking advantage of the strengths of others as well by delegating and outsourcing tasks whenever necessary. You are building up your business. Every single step that you take is one that is based solely on the vision for your business.

What Exactly Do You Vision?

If you have been following this book as was suggested in the introduction, you should have already written down your meaning of success.

If you have yet to do this, you may want to consider going back to the introduction section and then take this important step. Without this, the next step will be very difficult for you to complete.

A vision is simply what you desire for your business. This is not the same as your business' mission statement, which will be discussed next. The vision for your business is all about you. This statement is one that specifies what you would like your business to become.

A vision statement can provide you with answers to the following:

- What product or service is your business offering?
- Who are your customers?

- Does your business target a specific region?

A vision statement should always be written in the present tense. Although you may be looking into the future, it should be written as if it were happening right at this moment.

The vision statement that you create should also be emotional. Keep in mind that this is all about your definition of success. If you are not passionate or emotional about the idea, you cannot expect anyone else to share that same fire.

Lastly, your vision should be one that is detailed and descriptive. Add as many details as you dream up. Remember that this is not an actual test, and there is no right or wrong answers. A vision statement is highly personal. Begin by writing out a rough draft of the statement. You can go back and refine it to make it perfectly match your vision.

One Example Of A Vision Statement

Our Vision

A vision is the necessary guide which leads every detail of the business by outlining a plan of attack which must be followed in order to achieve sustainable growth.

- **Staff:** To be a workplace where people look forward to their work day and want to share their inspirations with others.

- **Network:** Creating a cohesive relationship between those that supply product and those that purchase products. By creating value, these life sources will feel appreciated and continue the cycle.

- **Products:** Providing customers with a generous product line that offers both quantity and quality.

Financial: Providing positive return for those with a financial stake in the company.

Always remember that your personal vision will serve as the groundwork for your business. This will serve as the tool that you use to measure your success and the tool that you will use to make your business decisions. Creating your vision statement is an extremely important part of the process. Keep in mind that you can change your vision if you like. It is not set in stone.

Take the time to sit down and write your vision statement

Now is the time to take a moment and write down your vision statement. If you already have your success definition written down, you may refer to it for guidance. It may help you create a great beginning.

Vision Statement Writing Tips

Try not to stress out about this task. Remember this is supposed to be a fun activity. Just allow yourself to start writing. Nothing is set in stone, so it is okay if you wind up kicking your original vision statement to the curb. The process of actually writing your thoughts and your vision down on paper will bring you just one step closer to the final statement.

Create a list. For some, writing one or two descriptive paragraphs can be difficult. Instead, create a list that answers the questions that were listed in the, "What Exactly Is Your Vision?" section. Who is your target customer? What products and/or services are you offering? How are you different from your competition? Continue this list by stating what you want your business to look like. After the list is complete, you can go back and place it into paragraph format and infuse your passion into it.

Creating a vision statement for your business is an extremely important step and one that you cannot skip. Just pause for a moment and contemplate how a business would be successful without utilizing a vision statement. There are many businesses that do and they usually do not go far. How would you make decisions about hiring new employees, marketing or the creation of a business model without even knowing what you want your business to be? You simply cannot do this.

The vision that you have for your business serves as the foundation for your success. This is the place where you will begin building your blueprint to riches. Along with your business' mission statement, you will have everything that you need to create an online business that is not only successful, but sustainable as well.

Mission Statement

Your mission statement is a separate statement from your vision statement. As the name implies, your mission statement refers to your customer and what your business is striving to do. This statement is just as crucial as a vision statement. It will serve as a guide for both you and those who are supporting your business to ensure that your customers are receiving what is promised.

Your mission statement will achieve the following:

- Define what makes your business stand out in the crowd
- Define what you are offering to your customers
- Define what your business model is

- Define your ideal customers

This may sound complicated, but it really is not.

One Example Of A Mission Statement

Our Mission

Our mission is to provide extraordinary customized service to each client that walks through our doors. Each decision that is made and carried out will be with a blanket approach that substantiates and adheres to our mission.

- To off the client a whole body approach that is unique and inspiring
- To set a gold standard by which others recognize our brand

To create an ambiance that is refreshing, joyful and fosters goal attainment

Just like a vision statement, it may be helpful to create a list. Consider the following when creating your mission statement:

- Your aspirations for your business' profitability and growth
- The moral and ethical position of your business
- The public image you want your business to have

It is important to remember that your mission statement is all about your customers. All of your promotions, marketing campaigns and sales strategies need to be uniformly working towards one goal. At the same time, your mission statement also needs to adhere to your vision statement as well. The vision and mission statement of a company work hand in hand to shape the business. They act as a compass to guide you while creating your blueprint to riches.

Create Your Mission Statement

Hopefully, you have been documenting your progress thus far. No matter whether you are taking this action by using a voice recorder or typing it up on your computer, it is time to create your mission statement. This first draft of your statement probably is not being posted up on your website (and that is okay). This is only for your eyes right now. Be as creative as you want and brainstorm away. In fact, write as many statements as you desire. You will know when you have finally captured it.

Creating Your Blueprint

Within this chapter, you have created your own definition for success, a vision statement and a mission statement. Great work! These are the first steps in creating the foundation for your business. The following chapters are a bit shorter and focus greatly on vital concepts that help create and grow a business that is profitable. Each of these chapters will discuss a particular business concept that will help you in creating your blueprint.

Put That Train Into Motion

Much of this book focuses on planning. After all, you cannot take action if you do not have direction or a goal that you are reaching towards. At the same time, you will never reach the goals you create and obtain the wealth you desire if you only have a blueprint.

Taking Action Is Key

Planning is the easy part for many people. They can continuously plan one successful business after another and are wonderful planners. What stops them from reaching their goals and finding success is that they never take action.

In reality, plans are merely words written on paper. They are not what create your business. The actions that you take are what create your business. In fact, *you* are the very heart and soul of your business.

Of course, you also have people who are great at taking action. They find an opportunity and dive right in. All this does is create results that are inconsistent and never really have a focus. The opportunities may produce profits, but if actions are being taken without the individual having any kind of vision or plan for success, they are never going to last. A blueprint to riches is designed to help you create success that is not only sustainable, but long lasting as well.

Well, if it is not enough to plan or to take action, then what is the solution?

Taking Inspired Action

The term "inspired action" refers to taking action that supports your goals and your vision. This is the reason why you are creating your blueprint. Every single aspect of the journey you take will be based on your vision. Every single action that you take will be inspired by your passions, your definition of success and your vision. This is not to say that you cannot take any actions that are not in your strategic plans. It is important, however, to determine whether that action will support your vision.

For instance, let's imagine that you are creating a business where you write and sell rock climbing travel guides. The vision that you have for your business is to create guides for every single destination, no matter how large or small. You want to be known as the best rock climbing travel guide resource there is. How you define this success is by traveling the world exploring and investigating these destinations. All the while, you make use of a team and current technology to streamline the marketing of the guides, sales and fulfillment tasks for your business.

After gaining some recognition for your efforts, a manufacturer of rock climbing equipment approaches you and extends a partnership offer. In return for promoting their products, you receive a percentage of the profits. Your first reaction may be to immediately jump on board, or you may be quick to say "no thanks". Once you investigate the opportunity further, you see that this partnership may be able to help you realize your vision far more quickly and allow you to have the income you need to outsource even more tasks or to travel more. Conversely, promoting these products may wind up taking up more resources than you prefer to allocate and you may determine that this is not a great opportunity for you.

It is important to take the time to do a careful and thorough analysis of every single action that you take to ensure that it is in line with your vision. This will keep you on the steady path towards success.

It is your goal to take inspired action. While you are creating or fine tuning your business, try to make it a habit to ask yourself, "Will this action support the vision that I have for my business?"

Is It Better To Take Small Steps Or Big Leaps?

Much like how there are people who prefer to plan rather than take action or those that opt to take action instead of planning, there are also some people who prefer to take smaller steps and some who prefer to take giant leaps.

It really does not matter what your preference is. What matters is that you recognize what your action-taking personality is and you plan accordingly.

Taking Action With Small Steps

For most people, setting larger goals like starting up a new business or reaching a million dollars in sales is easier to achieve when broken down into smaller steps. This is an excellent strategy and helps make the process far more manageable. It is much easier to say, "Today, I am going to write my sales letter" than it is to say "I am going to make one million dollars."

As you begin to create your blueprint and develop strategies that will allow you to realize your vision, it is crucial that you set goals for yourself. At the same time, you will need to implement systems that help you collect data and measure your success. We will go into further detail about these systems, operating procedures and metrics in Chapter 8. Just know that in order for you to develop your goals and the strategies to attain those goals, you really need to know your personality and the way you take on goals.

If you find that it is much easier and less stressful to take smaller steps, then that is how you should create your plan.

Taking Big Leaps

There are some people who just love to dive right into new opportunities. These people would much rather reach their goals right now then wait for tomorrow. It is important to choose whatever works best for you. Just as with those who like to take smaller steps, it is important that you first determine your personality and then make plans that suit that personality.

Let's say that your goal is to forge a partnership with another business that is complementary to yours. This can really be accomplished in one day through first planning and brainstorming, then researching, and then finally calling the business partner you have in mind. If you are the type of person who prefers to take smaller steps, this is a process that could take weeks or even months. That is perfectly acceptable as well.

The most important thing that you need to keep in mind is that if you create a business plan that is not in line with your personality and the way that you normally do things, you will not find success. You have to use your strengths to your advantage if you wish to really build a business plan and follow through in a profitable way.

Getting Out Of Your Comfort Zone

Every once in awhile, you may find a goal that you are compelled to take on in a different way. For example, you may be a person who normally prefers to take baby steps, but feels inspired to take on this particular goal right away. Go with your instincts. Just recognize that this is different from your normal way of doing things and go with it. There is a reason why we have these impulses and why we often regret it if we do not follow them. If you feel compelled to go outside of your comfort zone, then go for it.

If you truly want to realize your dream, see your definition of success come to light and make your vision a reality, you need to take inspired action. Without inspired action, or taking any kind of action that is guided by a plan, your business will remain nothing more than a dream that is written on a piece of paper.

Simple Practice:

How would you define your action taking personality?

Are you a person that works better when you take small steps towards your goal, or do you prefer to take big leaps? If you are not sure of how to answer this question, you may want to take a closer look at your past successes. How did you prefer to tackle those bigger goals in life? Were you the type of person who simply dove right in, or did you break it down into smaller and more manageable tasks? There really is nothing to write down with this particular exercise unless you feel compelled to do so. Just make note of how you prefer to set and attain goals so that you can remember this when it does come time to take action.

What Part Are You Playing?

In Michael Gerber's famous books The E-Myth and The E-Myth Revisited, he pinpoints three crucial roles that all entrepreneurs use in their business. Gerber defines the E-Myth as the faulty assumption that a person who is a master of a particular skill will be highly successful running a business in an industry related to that skill.

For instance, if you happen to be a great artist, then you will automatically find great success by opening and running your own art business. Let's say that you are a skilled software designer. According to Michael Gerber you will find that opening and running your own software design business will automatically provide you with success.

It is important to understand that in order to own a business, you must take on many different roles.

On top of being the writer or the designer, for example, you must also be the business' visionary and the one that steers the business in the right direction. In the beginning, you will also be the person who makes phone calls, answers emails and takes on all of the daily administrative tasks. You are also the one who has to coordinate these tasks.

An entrepreneur is:

- The CEO
- The Creative Thinker
- The Administrator
- The Fix It Person
- The Sales Team
- The Advertising Team

And so on and so forth.

It is crucial that you understand what your strengths are simply because you are required to take on so many different roles. Once you have determined which tasks you excel in, you can outsource or find ways to automate the other tasks. This will allow you to have more time to build a business that embodies all that you are passionate about and skilled at. It allows you to have the time to remain the visionary of the company. This means that you can take on the tasks that help generate profits and outsource all of the tasks that just steals your precious time. We will further discuss time management in Chapter 7.

What Are Your Personal Strongholds?

If you know what you are really good at, then you know where you should be focusing your time and your energy. If you happen to be an excellent web designer, then designing websites is what you should be doing. Why is this? Simply because being skilled at and passionate about something will bring you rewards both financially and personally. If you wind up spending your days working on tasks that you are not skilled at, you will wind up becoming unproductive and will likely find your job to be unfulfilling. You will not be focusing your time and efforts into something that is pleasurable, profitable and productive.

When you can focus on your strengths, you are able to receive significant rewards. The results of your hard work are far more profitable. You will also feel both proud and accomplished as a result. The rewards are not only profitable but they also provide you with personal pleasure. This is the all important reason why you run your own business. It allows you to understand where your strengths are and leverage them. In addition, it also allows you to compensate for your weaknesses.

How Do You Handle those Tasks That You Lack The Skills?

Once you understand and accept what your weaknesses are, you are actually providing yourself with more options than you think. How you handle the tasks that you are not skilled with is entirely up to you. You can choose to hire someone who is an expert in these tasks. You could also ask someone else for some help or advice. Or, you may even schedule one day to take care of all of these tasks yourself. The choice is yours.

How you choose to delegate these tasks is up to you. The important thing is that you understand what your weaknesses are so that you can make your decisions appropriately. If you simply cannot grasp the concept of a particular programming language, then why would you sit in front of your computer for hours on end trying to learn it? You are only torturing yourself and wasting time. The end result is not going to be exactly how you envisioned it. If you were to hire someone who is skilled in this field, they will be able to complete the job much quicker and for less money than what it is costing you in time and sanity.

Exercise:

How can your strengths be applied to your business?

Let's say that you are a wonderful musician. Unless you are planning on selling products online, this really is not a strength that can be applied to your internet business. However, if you are great at communicating with others and setting goals, these strengths can be applied to a business where you provide online coaching sessions for those who want to pursue their dream job.

The point here is that when you realize what your strengths are, you can focus your time and energy on these things and work on improving them. Remember, your strengths are what will help you to find success.

Bridging The Gap Between What You Love And Making Others Love It Too

Loving What You Do Or Passion: The One Important Ingredient In The Creation And Management Of A Business

Is it possible to have a business without any passion? Of course it is. There are many people that do. Just imagine, however, getting up every morning and feeling miserable about having to go to work. This is probably not too hard for many people to imagine. Perhaps that is how you feel right now. It can be very difficult to obtain wealth if you are unmotivated about running your business. Without any passion, your motivation takes a long vacation.

On the other hand, if you are truly passionate about what you are doing and it is fun for you, not only will you be motivated to get up and go to work, but you will also be able to motivate others as well. Happiness and passion are two emotions that are highly contagious. When you are passionate about what you are doing, you will feel inspired and you will be amazed at the partnerships and ideas that will come your way. This will allow you to build up your business far more quickly and you will see much greater success when you have passion.

It is true that the term "passion" is a word that is used far too often, and you may have rolled your eyes when you heard the term being used here. The word passion has really taken on a frilly or even silly connotation.

There are a number of different synonyms for the word passion. Zeal, enthusiasm, fervor, excitement and spirit are just a few. If you prefer, you can use any one of these words in place of the term passion. The point is that you need to base your business on something that you will be happy to get out of the bed in the morning to do. You should be excited about it and be eager to share this excitement with others every single day. Ask yourself this question, if you started up a conversation in the grocery store with a complete stranger, would you be enthusiastic about sharing your business with them?

If you have already started your business and you chose to focus on something that you really are not passionate about, it may be time for you to take a step backward and re-evaluate things. Why did you choose this particular niche and business model? What do you feel your business is lacking? Do you think it may be possible to find that passion or create it for your particular niche or business model? Or, do you think you may be better off going with a new niche and new business model? Follow your gut. You may even be able to transform your current business into something for which you have passion.

If you are just starting up your business, you probably have already come up with a few different ideas on what your business niche will be and which model you are going to follow. You may have even performed some research to make sure that it is a business idea that is worth pursuing. If you have not done any of these things, you may want to do a personal analysis and a little brainstorming. Start by creating a list of things that you are passionate about and then brainstorm some ideas for a possible business.

For instance, if you were really passionate about dog training, you could create dog training guides for new pet owners. You could also sell products that would be useful for training or offer private coaching sessions. If you are certified, you can even offer training sessions. If you would prefer to stay out of the spotlight, you could create a community through a membership site that is dedicated to dog training. There are so many different options for just about every niche.

The next thing that you need to do is size up your competition in the niche that you choose and analyze the idea. Will you be able to create a mission and a vision statement that is based on this niche and the model that you have chosen? If you are able to, you are definitely on the right track.

Remember that passion plays a crucial role in the creation of your blueprint to success. If you start out your journey without any passion, you will be quick to avoid your work. You will find yourself always being distracted, neglecting your business and all of the decisions that you make will wind up being a mere effort to find some kind of meaning in your business instead of remaining focused on your final goal and your vision.

The Great Marketing Myth

There are many people that grit their teeth when they hear the 'M' word. The concept of marketing makes a lot of people really uncomfortable. They just imagine themselves having to make cold calls, resorting to manipulative tactics in their sales letters and all of the other tactics that salesmen are known for. Thankfully, true marketing is far different than this terrible myth.

Think about your favorite subject; something that you know a lot about and are naturally interested in. If you were to discuss this topic with someone at a party, you would be enthusiastic. You would naturally be energetic. Hopefully, the person that you are speaking with is just as interested in what you are saying as you are discussing it. This is really what marketing is.

Marketing Is Simply Sharing Your Passion With Those Who Are Interested

Do you have to be passionate about your business to market it? It certainly does give you a major advantage.

- If you enjoy what you are doing and are excited about your work, you will find that sharing your vision with employees, team members, vendors, contractors, partners, etc. comes naturally.
- Enthusiasm and passion are highly contagious
- It will be easier for you to take action that is inspired
- It will be easier to plan for the future

So, You Are Passionate About Your Business. Great! Now What Do You Do?

Having passion is a great place to start. You have the determination and the enthusiasm to develop a marketing and sales plan that you can really stand behind.

The success of your business will rest solely on your marketing efforts. If you do not implement some kind of marketing strategy, how can you expect people to know that you are offering products or services? If you do not market your business, you will never have customers. Furthermore, you will never have any repeat customers. Marketing truly is the driving force behind your business. This is especially true if you are just starting up your business.

Developing a marketing strategy is an effective and integral part of your business and also your role as being an entrepreneur. In fact, this is such an important part of the success of your business (not to mention it is valuable) that many great business men and women believe it should be the primary concern for a business owner. An effective marketing strategy is crucial to the profitability and the success of your business.

In order to truly create a successful marketing strategy, you must understand your target audience. Why are they buying? How can your product fill a purpose in their lives? How can your services or products better their lives? What is your unique selling proposition?

How Is Your Business Different?

This is what is referred to as your USP or your *unique selling proposition*. This often comes in the form of a tagline or as a slogan. These sentences describe what makes you different from your competition. Think about some of the brands with which you are most familiar. There is a good chance that you can also recall their slogan. Take a moment to think about how that slogan works to set them apart from others in their industry.

Practice:

Ponder those things that give your business that extra edge when it comes to competitors. What is it about your USP that sets you apart from others? Contemplate the ways that your customers will benefit from your service or your products.

Here is the only catch: your USP needs to be centered on what your customers really care about and need. It is important to be different and unique, but this is not enough to draw in customers. Through your USP, you must communicate the ways that your business is unique in a format that is important to your potential customers.

Developing A Marketing Strategy

A good marketing strategy will allow you to focus more on your business while these systems that you have implemented will sell your services or products for you.

What the marketing process includes is:

- Conducting market research to determine what services or products customers really want
- Developing a product that matches quality and features that customers need

- Determining the right price for the product

- Getting the word out about the product and why customers need to buy it
- Finalizing the sale and distributing the product to the customer's hands

What To Consider When Developing A Marketing Strategy

1. Start out by describing your business in one simple and short paragraph. What is your mission statement? In other words, what is your business' purpose? Furthermore, what is the name of the company and how do you plan on accommodating the market?

2. What is your target market? Make a list of your ideal customer's psychographics and demographics. This includes their wants, their personality traits and their habits.

3. What is your goal for your marketing efforts? What is your end game?

4. What advantage do you have over your competitors? What is it about your company that makes it stand out in the crowd? How will this advantage help support your success?

5. Who is your target audience?

6. What strategies and tools will you use in your marketing efforts?

7. What is your position in the market?

8. What does your budget look like?

If you are truly passionate about your industry or niche, marketing becomes a task that is both exciting and profitable. This is more than just manipulating people and convincing them to buy your products or services. Instead, you share valuable information and your own knowledge about what you are offering. You share details about how the product or service can really benefit their lives. This is effective marketing.

Before you can really begin marketing your products, you need to first learn more about your target audience. What are their fears, wants and hopes? What is it that your audience needs? Is there a way that you can position your business to provide your audience with what they need? This is the very heart of marketing.

Focus: What Is Your Unique Blueprint?

When you hear the term "business plan", what comes to mind?

Chances are your vision includes a business man or woman dressed in a suit spending hours leaning over their computer or notebook. Business plans are complex and require a great deal of work, right? Most people just assume that they will need the financial expertise of Warren Buffet to successfully create their business plan.

Unfortunately, traditional business plans have developed a bad reputation.

At the same time, it would be insensible to start up a business without such a plan. The good news is that unless you will be seeking out funding from investors or applying for a business loan, you really do not have to create a traditional business plan.

Instead, you can create a blueprint.

What Exactly Is A Blueprint?

A blueprint is, essentially, a business plan for you and not the bankers. It encompasses your vision, your passion and your mission statement. It also includes your plan on how to reach your goals.

Why create a blueprint? Much like the development of a building, there are a number of changes made before the final structure is complete. Some new opportunities may arise, new technology may be developed and your vision may change along the way. The blueprint you create will provide you with some direction while also allowing you to make some modifications along the way. As your business continues to grow and change, your blueprint will need to change as well.

When you develop a blueprint for your business, you provide yourself with something you can turn to every single day for direction, inspiration and motivation. It also allows you to:

- Create new strategies that help you maintain your success
- Accomplish your goals quickly
- Stay on the right track
- Create the wealth that you desire

Crucial Components For A Successful Business Plan

Vision Statement

In the first chapter, we discussed the importance of a vision statement. This is what defines what your business is and what direction it is headed in.

When you create a vision statement that is effective, you will find it much easier to stay on track. Your vision statement is your plan for your company's future. It is also what you will use to analyze your strategies and determine whether or not they will help you get there.

Mission Statement

Your business' mission statement defines its purpose. It is precise, to the point and declares what your company's purpose is. It declares your reason for existing. While your vision statement is all about your own personal goals and vision for the company, the mission statement is all about what your customers are looking for.

Your company's mission statement should be focused on the present moment and the direction that your company is presently moving. Your mission statement should be written in the present tense and focus on the current moment.

Developing Strategies

In order to realize the goals written in your vision and mission statements, you need to develop strategies for every single area of your business. For instance, you will need to create strategies for marketing and product development.

When you begin the process of creating your strategies, ask yourself the following questions:

1. Is this strategy in line with my company's mission and vision?

2. Will this plan help me receive the highest possible return on my investment? (This includes time and energy as well as money.)

3. Is this strategy profitable? If so, will the profits be long term and sustainable? Furthermore, is the strategy enjoyable for me?

Goals

Each time you develop a new strategy, you have a goal in mind. Goals are measurable outcomes that can be used to gauge your success. For instance, an example goal is to develop and release four informational products this year.

Every little aspect of your business needs to have a strategy. Naturally, every strategy needs to have a goal. Creating a detailed and structured plan that also includes plans on how to measure success will allow you to reach your goals quickly.

Do Not Leave Your Blueprint On The Shelf

You are an entrepreneur. You need to maintain your role as the visionary for your business. It is very easy to get bogged down by the menial day-to-day tasks involved with running a business. When this happens, be aware as the company can start falling off track. At this point, you begin to lose profit and time. Thankfully, there is a way to quickly get you back on the right track.

Take the time to really analyze your business and the plan you have created on a regular basis. Whether it is monthly, weekly or quarterly, you need to find time to plan. In order to prevent procrastination or creation of excuses, you should ensure that your plan is in a format that is easily accessible. If you do the majority of your work on your laptop, make sure that you have a copy of your plan saved to your desktop. If you prefer to write your plans down on paper, be sure to keep your documentation in a place that is easy and convenient for you to access.

Because inspirations can arise at any time, you may want to keep a notebook or a voice recorder nearby so you can take advantage of the moment and record your ideas. You then have the freedom to go back at a later day and analyze those ideas during your planning sessions.

During your planning sessions, be sure to analyze whether or not the modifications you are considering will actually support your vision and your business. If you find that they do not support your vision, then you may want to reconsider adapting them.

Choosing A Profitable Business Model

There are plenty of business models out there, but which one is right for you? This will depend on what your vision is, how much time you can put into your business, what is your chosen niche and an outline of your goals. Below are a few different business models from which you can choose:

1. Product Based Business
2. Information Marketing
3. Serviced Based Business
4. Membership Sites

Product Based Business

A product based business is one that you are likely very familiar with already. It involves the selling or wholesaling of physical products. If you have the talent and vision, you can create your own products as well. In fact, Etsy.com is now the most popular online marketplace for the sale of handmade goods. There are more than one hundred thousand sellers on the website from all over the world.

Information Marketing

Information marketing is better understood as the selling of digital products. This particular business model is one that is growing exponentially and showing no signs of slowing.

Information marketers sell the following products:

- Online Courses
- Coaching Sessions
- eBooks
- Software
- Videos

Any and all downloadable content can be sold under this business model. What you choose to sell will depend upon your own personal strengths, the niche you choose and the passions which drive you.

If you are not too keen on the idea of creating your own informational products, you have the option of purchasing resale rights to books that others have already written. On the other hand, you may find yourself a good ghostwriter to create the books for you. The greatest advantage to selling information products is that the business essentially runs itself once you have your system set up and automated. This will then leave you with plenty of time to create more products, continue to grow your business and focus on other things that are a part of your definition of success.

Service Based Business

As far as online services are concerned, professional coaching is by far the most common service available. Coaches can provide their services via email, over the telephone or through Skype sessions. Graphic design, writing, consulting, administrative services and programming are other common services offered online.

To determine whether or not a service based business would work best for you, consider the following questions:

- Are you an expert in a particular niche or area of interest?
- Do you like to work with people?
- Is there a market for your specialized knowledge?

Membership Sites

An informational or membership site is another profitable and popular business model, but they generate income in different ways. A membership site profits from the sales of memberships or subscriptions. These sites attract people that are interested in a particular service, information or product. An informational website makes a profit through selling advertising space on the website. There is also a great deal of money to be made through affiliate marketing. This involves the sale and promotion of products from other companies.

There are no limitations here either. You can choose a number of different combinations. A service based business can promote products or sell products as well. A product based business can also provide their customers with services. When you create your blueprint, it is important that you have some kind of framework in mind. Of course, this does not mean that everything must be set in stone. Things can change and grow over time. When your business begins to grow and evolve, you may see a demand for certain services or products that were not a part of your original plans. If you do decide to offer new products or services, you will need to make changes to your business plan and model. Therefore, it is important to ensure that these changes support your company's mission and vision.

Capturing A Customer Following That Will Come Aboard Forever

In order to build a business that is truly profitable, you must build a list. This is the single most important tool for a business to have. To put it simply, a list is a database of potential or current customers that are interested in the information, services or products that you offer.

Once you start gaining traffic, or visitors, to your site, the next goal is to entice them to share their contact information. Oftentimes, this is done by offering something in return for the information. For instance, many people offer free reports, books, seminars or videos. Whatever it is your offer, it needs to be valuable to the person.

What are some things that your audience will value? This is where a little market research comes in. By now, you likely already know your audience. What is it that they need? What do they really want? The goal is to find a way to give these things to them.

The end game here is to get your visitors to sign up and become a part of your list. This is done using a few different tactics and strategies, which may include:

1. Social Marketing and Networking: Becoming an active member of industry-related forums, social networking websites, blogs and other platforms that are relevant to your niche.

2. SEO: Linking, tagging and adding valuable content on a regular basis.

3. Affiliates: Developing a program where other marketers can promote your services or products in exchange for an incentive or commission.

4. Advertising: Purchasing search engine advertising space through Google's AdWords, advertising space on industry-related websites or networking with others to cross promote.

So now that you have traffic coming in to your website and you have started to build up your list, what is the next step?

It is essential that you regularly communicate with your customers and those on your opt-in list. Generally speaking, you should have a ratio of eighty percent information and twenty percent marketing. The information that you offer will need to be valuable and beneficial to users. Marketing can be used to promote your products and services. This is where your marketing funnel will come in handy.

Marketing Funnel? What Is that?

In order to really make the most out of the relationship you develop between you and your customers, you need to create an experience that is valuable to your customers. More often than not, entrepreneurs find that creating a product line, or a "product funnel" works best.

In case you are unfamiliar, a product funnel is a line of products where the prices gradually increase. Think about a funnel. The largest portion is at the top and the smallest point is at the bottom.

Your clients will enter the funnel through the widest portion. Here, you may offer a trial version of your product or services, or you may offer a free product. You may also offer a low priced product as well. At the bottom of your funnel, you will offer your most expensive product. The logic here is that prospects will be much easier for your potential customers to make a purchasing decision if the financial commitment is very little or none at all. You will find that people are more willing to enter your funnel as a result.

Here is how the concept works:

1. The first step in the process is to convert a prospect into a client through the sale of a product or service. This can be a product at any level in your funnel.

2. At this stage you want to upsell your client. The goal is to convince them to buy the next highest priced item in your funnel. This is often referred to as a back-end sale.

   For instance, have you heard the phrase "Do you want some fries with that?" when going through the drive through? In this example, the fries are considered the back-end sale. If you fail to include a back-end sale in your business model, then you are essentially leaving money out on the table.

3. At this point, you want to continue offering customers and those on your opt-in list the other items in your funnel. This same pattern should continue on until the client decides that they no longer want to buy from you. If you continue to offer new products that are valuable to your customers, the funnel will last a long time.

When you offer product lines at different price levels, you make sure that every single client walks away happy. It also ensures that you make the highest profit possible with each client. At the end of the day, it is really all about customer service.

Keeping Customers Coming Back For More

Many people are under the false impression that you can just put up a website and start making millions of dollars. Sure, you may be able to attract a lot of attention to the site, but in order to create a business that is successful and long lasting, you need to provide:

- Something that is unique. This may be a product, an experience or a service.
- A customer experience that is memorable
- Authenticity and transparency

Earlier, we talked about USP, or what makes you different. This can be a variety of different things. Maybe you are offering a product or service that is very specific and unique. Perhaps the customer experience that you provide is different in some way. This can also include the customer experience at your website and your online communication with them as well.

People purchase products from people and companies that they like. The more they like a company or a person, the more they continue to buy from them. Who is it exactly that people like? More often than not, people like to purchase from retailers that like them and treat them very well. People also tend to gravitate towards companies and individuals that have a very distinct brand or personality.

As the owner of a small business, your own personality is your brand. When you think about it, this is often the case with owners of large businesses as well. Think about Martha Stewart, Donald Trump and Jeff Bezos. Each one has a very distinct personality and brand.

For internet entrepreneurs, it is critical not to get lost in the anonymity that the web offers. Always be transparent and always be genuine. Allow your customers to get to know your personality.

Membership sites and forums are an excellent way to do this. Either one of these platforms will provide you the opportunity to connect with customers and potential customers on a more personal level.

If you can find blogs that allow for interactive and two-way conversations, this is another great way to connect with your target audience. Sending email messages and newsletters to your potential customers is another route to take. Just make sure that you have a message that is distinct and purposeful to those who are reading your content.

In recent years, both audio and video have become extremely important tools for business owners to help them communicate with their audience. Many people are taking advantage of article and video marketing. It allows them to show their audience who they are and the definition basis of their company. At the same time, the content benefits the audience.

If you wish to really create and maintain loyal customers, you need to build up your relationship with them. The focus should really not be on the sales. They key is to provide your customers and potential customers with value. Regular communication with your audience is also crucial. Make them see that what you are offering will help solve their problem and better their lives.

Establishing Leaders

How Much Is Your Time Worth?

Whether you like it or not, there are only 24 hours in one day, 168 hours in every week and 365 days each year. No matter how hard you try, it just seems as if there is never enough time to get everything done. There are some people, however, who seem to be able to take on the world and do so with ease. How are these people able to accomplish so much in the same amount of time? Do they not sleep? Every person has the same amount of time, but it is what you do with your time that really counts.

Before we can really delve into ways to help you better manage your time, it is important that you understand how valuable your time is. Complete the following exercise first before you can determine the best way to spend your time.

Take a look at your hourly value. If you find that it is far less than you would like it to be, and chances are it is, then you are likely spending far too much time taking on tasks that are unprofitable. This includes answering emails and bookkeeping. If you really want to increase your hourly value and profits, you need to start focusing instead on tasks that are profit generating.

Let us take a look at better ways to manage your time so that you can finally reach your revenue target. This will make each day more enjoyable, more productive and far more profitable.

The Secret To Managing Your Time Effectively

In order to be effective, you need to get the most important things done first. The late and great Gary Halbert, who was considered one of the best copywriters in the world, would lock himself in his office and simply ignore everything else that was going on the other side of it.

It did not matter if the world was in chaos outside of his door. Mr. Halbert would simply ignore all of it. He was completely aware of the fact that his copywriting skills were his greatest strength and what would ultimately generate profits. So, this is what he focused on.

How on earth was he able to do this? For one thing, he had a staff that could handle any problems that may have popped up. He knew what his strengths were and he hired other people to take care of everything else.

Spending your time focusing on tasks that will generate a profit will improve your hourly rate exponentially. This is absolutely imperative for internet entrepreneurs who wish to make their business profitable. So, what do you do about all of the tasks that do not generate profits?

Taking Advantage Of Technology, Outsourcing And Delegating Tasks

A great thing about owning an online based business is that you will have access to a wide range of services and products needed to make an online business more profitable and efficient. Today, you can have email responses that are automated. This saves hours each day. A shopping cart system will create detailed reports. These reports can help you stay on top of sales trends and your inventory. Special membership software programs can take care of the billing and virtually everything else. Not only will this save you time, but it will also improve the user's experience, which is of the utmost importance.

Take a look at what tasks you can automate, so that you can start eliminating them from your to-do list.

The next thing you should focus on is the tasks that you can outsource. When you outsource, you hire freelancers or contractors to accomplish a variety of processes and tasks within the business. This will provide you with a chance to empty your plate of tasks that may be necessary for your business to operate but need not be completed by you.

Below are some tasks that are commonly outsourced and affordable:

- Content creation
- Transcription
- Copywriting
- Bookkeeping
- Scheduling
- Customer service
- Affiliate management
- Shipping and receiving

There are so many other tasks that you can outsource as well.

It is possible to find a number of qualified contractors and freelancers online. Bookkeepers, researchers, virtual assistants, graphic designers, web designers and even freelance writers all can be found online through a number of freelance websites like guru.com or elance.com. If you have connections with other entrepreneurs in the business, you can ask them for some referrals or recommendations. This will help ensure that you are hiring someone that is qualified and produces great work.

It is easy to go overboard in this department, so before you start outsourcing everything, you should take a step back and look at where your budget stands.

Take into consideration how long each task takes and then determine what your hourly value really is. Will you be able to hire someone to carry out the task at a much lower rate than your own hourly value? If so, then go ahead and outsource if it fits into your budget. If not, you may want to consider developing an outsourcing strategy and then adding it to your blueprint. This will ensure that you have some goals and a way to measure success so that you can determine when you will be able to afford to outsource services. This will also help you determine which task to outsource first.

When you reach a point where you can start outsourcing, it is critical that you have an in-depth job description available in writing. You must also provide a standard operating procedure to your contractor as well. Providing your contractor with a detailed and complete job description will ensure that the communication and expectations are clear. You should also devise a system for each responsibility. The clearer the communication is between you and your contractor, the better your relationship will be.

Forging partnerships is another excellent way to offset some of your responsibilities. For instance, if you know someone that is a wonderful marketer and you are a wonderful writer, you could offer to write content for him or for her in return for help with marketing your business. Again, this will require that you create a clear agreement up front and all communication should be direct and concise.

You must understand the value of your time in order to truly grow your business. This will allow you to make wise decisions on where to spend your time. There are many people that truly believe they can take on all of the tasks themselves. The truth is that they cannot. Even if you could take on everything yourself, why would you want to? Instead, focus your time on your strengths and on the tasks that generate you profits. Let others take care of everything else.

Company Goals: Setting And Fulfilling

In earlier chapters, we discussed the different aspects of a business plan. We talked about your mission statement, objectives and your vision statement. As you may remember, objectives are goals that are measurable. Examples include:

- I want to use this promotion to attain a 5% conversion rate.

- I want to increase my sales by 30% this year.

- I want to increase the number of subscribers to my list by 10% this quarter.

Every objective that you create needs to have a goal and it also needs to have a date to accomplish that goal. You can certainly create measurable objectives for your return rates, your customer service and the cost you incur per customer. However, it is the marketing goals that tend to receive the most attention. This is mainly because you would have no business without marketing.

All the same, your marketing can only be as good as the results it produces. You may believe that you have written the best sales letter, email campaign or promotion, but if your efforts are not turning your prospects into customers, then they are not even worth the paper they are written on. So, the question is: How can you know whether or not a piece really works? The answer is through testing.

There are two different types of testing that you can do. You can do multivariable testing and you can do split testing. Each one of these has their own set of pros and cons.

Split Testing

On paper, split testing seems rather simple. Let's say that you wanted to test the effectiveness of your newsletter sign up form. There are a number of different variables that may affect your sign up rates, including the body copy, the headline you use, the color of the form, your call to action, where the form is located or even the font that you choose. When utilizing the split testing method, you isolate each variable and then test it. For example, you could alter the form's location and then test its performance. This is sometimes referred to as A/B testing. To conduct the testing, you would create two separate home pages. One will have the form on the top right hand side of the page, while the other will be located in a completely different spot. Using the same techniques that you normally do to generate traffic to your site, you would then send some visitors to your standard home page and others to your test page.

When you do this correctly, you will receive data that is accurate and very beneficial. The biggest disadvantage to this form of testing is that it can take a great deal of time to actually accumulate the data. If you are only testing one variable at time, it can take even longer to really optimize your marketing strategy. Generally speaking, it will take fifty different actions to really provide you with data that is statistically relevant and you will be left with a margin of error of around twelve percent.

Multivariable Testing

With multivariable testing, you can make the testing process run much quicker. Of course, it is a bit more complex and is typically only used for online purposes. The measurements are usually centered on site statistics such as click through rates. The Taguchi Method is a popular multivariate testing method. While it may be true that multivariable testing can test many different aspects of a website at one time, it can still take a great deal of time to actually accumulate enough data to make informed decisions. This is especially true if a website has medium to low traffic.

Tools To Use For Testing

Many people are unsure of where to start when it comes to testing. Generally, basic testing is something that can be dealt with internally. This is something that you can do yourself, or you can hire another person to track the data for you and compile it. You can choose to take advantage of more advanced technology in this regard, or you can choose to use a simple Excel spreadsheet to track all of your marketing data.

There are many different online websites that can help with tracking. Google Analytics is a great example of a tool that can help you measure customer response to a number of different web pages. It can also help you track the click through rates of items that you are testing, such as your sign up form. Much like many other things, Google offers this service for free.

Many web hosts will also offer useful analytical tools that will allow you to keep track of relevant statistics. There are also a range of software programs and consulting firms that can help those that are interested in conducting split or multivariable testing.

Data Tracking

Many people have heard of tracking, but are unsure of what that actually means. To put it simply, you make use of the data available to determine how your prospects and your customers are responding to your business and your marketing efforts. You may want to track:

50

- How long your visitors are staying on your site
- How many visitors are choosing to opt-in
- How many pages your visitors are viewing before they leave your site
- How many visitors are purchasing your products
- How many items each customer is purchasing

Tracking will pinpoint the areas of your system that are working and the areas that are not working. Remember, tools like Google Analytics can really help you track a lot of data. Your shopping cart, or even your accounting software, will be able to help you track key information about your customer's purchases.

When you create your blueprint to riches, you should take the time to develop objectives that are measurable and then create a way to measure that success. When you have this information on hand, you will be better prepared to make important decisions that will push your business forward and in the right direction. This is why it is so important to not only create your blueprint, but also create a plan that can help you evaluate your blueprint frequently. This means evaluating whether or not you are attaining your objectives. If you are reaching your goals, then it is time to start creating new ones. If you are not attaining your goals, you can take advantage of tracking information and testing methods to determine why you are not succeeding. If you plan on making changes to your blueprint, always make sure that they are supporting your vision and your own definition of success.

You certainly did not go into business to become a slave to your work. You decided to go into business so that you could improve your life. Develop a plan that actually meets your needs, your personal definition of success and your greatest strengths. Analyze your plan on a regular basis. Be willing and able to adapt to new situations and implement new strategies in order to meet the demands of your customers. Take advantage of any opportunity that comes your way and is in line with your company's vision. Not only will you find yourself on the right path towards your goal, but you will reach your goal quicker than you ever imagined.

Exercise:

Sit down and write five goals for your business. Make sure to take into consideration how you are going to measure your success and think about what tools and/or resources you can use to test or track that data.

Well done!

You are now on your way to accomplishing all that you have envisioned for your business and for yourself.

Best of luck to you!